Whispers of the Twins
A Divination Companion

Tony Whitman

and

Jessica Tiderman

Sage & Hawthorn Print, LLP

Printed in the United States of America

ISBN 978-0-9960638-3-8

Sage & Hawthorn Print, LLP
www.sagehawthorn.com

Dedication

To our wonderfully fabulous children -
Thank you for cooperating with us and each other
and for tolerating us while we worked on this book.

CONTENTS

"She boils over with a tremendous fire, because she is full of your wrath, Apollo! You do not only use your whip on her and inject fire into her vitals as you goad her; she also feels your curb and as a prophetess she may not reveal as much as she is allowed to know. All time concentrates in one complex; all centuries descend upon her heart - poor woman - and the great chain of events lies open; the whole future struggles to come into the light; destinies fight destinies to be expressed in her voice. She sees everything; the first day and the last day of the world, the dimensions of the Ocean, the sum of the sands!"
Lucan, Pharsalia, 5.86 – 224

Georg Luck, *Arcana Mundi: Magic and the Occult in the Greek and Roman Worlds* (Baltimore: The John Hopkins University Press, 2006), 344.

This book honors the god of prophecy, Apollo, and his sister, Artemis.

Chapter 1
Purpose and Format

The role of this book is to function as a 'little white book' for all the divination systems that I use. Many systems such as the I Ching and Ifa are not here as those have their own oracles already. This book is an attempt to flesh out other divination systems so that they are more like the I Ching and Ifa systems. This is not an absolute model though, not all divination systems use this design.

The basic oracle structure is:

> Information: There is the influence of…
>   Followed by
> Suggested action: It would be wise to…

> Examples:
>   It's going to rain. You might want to get inside.
>   An extraordinary event is about to happen. You might want to ground yourself.

Divination can help people decide how they want to meet their fate. It can help people discover what hand they were dealt in life and how they may want to play it. No one can know all things, but one can know what their place is in a grander scheme. However, sometimes to know the future is to be trapped by it. Other times there is a ring of truth that can set you free. Seeking a balance can be very difficult.

There are other important attitudes to keep in mind about divination. Fate may tell us when and even how we are going to die, but it does not tell us how we choose to meet that death. We do not judge a poker player by the hand they are dealt, but how they play that hand. Divination is also about influences. These can be strengths, obstacles, gifts, or weaknesses. These are the core tenets of divination.

Tarot is communicating with the elements. Astrology is communication with the worlds of the higher universe. Dreams are conversations within the worlds of all other entities. There is an overlap, an abstract realm, that accesses all those realms. For the lack of a better word, I call this the Shadow World. This is where I went to create the oracles. The language should be outside of time and space, yet definitive.

Divination is not about seeing patterns in front of you, it's about the divination and those spiritual and magical patterns taking you somewhere else where you can see and plan with more clarity. It may help you ask the right question, which is better than most of the answers. An oracle is a combination of all your own understandings and is the mark of a seeker, a holder of the fire of Prometheus. Like the physician - divine thyself.

Chapter 2
The Six M's

These are the guidelines for the creation and use of the divination sets presented here.

1) Medium

This is the physical material that the divination set is made out of. It may also include what the mandala is made of, but not the pattern of the mandala.

Examples: bones, cards, a pendulum and a circle, dice on a board, tea leaves and water, coffee beans and water, planets, seashells and sand, coins and cloth, etc.

2) Method

This is how the medium is used.

Examples: to throw the dice, to observe the planets, to lay the cards, to swing the pendulum, to drop the shells on the sand, to draw a rune, etc.

3) Mandala

This is a pattern that can add further context to the divination.

Examples: solar system star map, tarot spread, a pentagram for bones, the indicator lines of a palm reading, etc.

4) Mythology

This is the cultural background that influences and develops the mode of communication. A mythological framework helps give added subtext and rich metaphorical examples.

Examples: chosen lines from the Iliad used as answers, the stanzas of an I Ching ideogram, the stanzas from the Norse Eddas.

5) Mode of Communication

This is how the medium "speaks" to the diviner.

Examples: stanzas, abstracts, associations, oracles.

6) Meaning

This is the interpretation of all the previous factors coming into play all at once. It includes the question and answers interplay.

The Astrological Example:

Medium: The Planets (and moons)
Method: The Orbits
Mandala: The Constellation Borders
Mythology: Greek
Mode of Communication: Oracles and Interactions
Meaning: The Interpretation

A divination set is thorough when all six M's are present, but it is by no means necessary and rarely the case. When developed, they help to create a powerful spiritual narrative to guide and illuminate.

Chapter 3
The GMP Homeric Oracles

Medium: Dice
Method: Throwing
Mandala: None
Mythology: Greek
Mode: Lines from the Iliad (*Il.*) and Odyssey (*Od.*)

Betz , Hans Dieter, *The Greek Magical Papyri in Translation* (Chicago: The University of Chicago Press, 1996), 112-118.

Omissions are to be translated as "*Unknown.*"

1. 1-1-1 But on account of their accursed bellies they have miserable woes, [*Od.* 15. 344]

2. 1-1-2 neither to cast anchor stones nor to attach stern cables, [*Od.* 9. 137]

3. 1-1-3 being struck by the sword, and the water was becoming red with blood. [*Il.* 21. 21]

4. 1-1-4 . . .

5. 1-1-5 stood holding a scepter, which Hephaistos produced by his labours. [*Il.* 2. 101]

6. 1-1-6 . . .

7. 1-2-1 amends I wish to make and to give a boundless ransom. [*Il.* 9. 120; 19. 138]

8. 1-2-2 surely then the gods themselves have ruined your mind. [*Il.* 7. 360; 12. 234]

9. 1-2-3 . . .

10. 1-2-4 . . .

11. 1-2-5 let it lie in the great hall. And I wish for your happy arrival [*Od.* 15. 128]

12. 1-2-6 . . .

13. 1-3-1 . . .

14. 1-3-2 . . .

15. 1-3-3 But Zeus does not accomplish for men all their purposes. [*Il.* 18. 328]

16. 1-3-4 I would even wish it, and it would be much better [*Il.* 3. 41; *Od.* 11. 358; 20. 316]

17. 1-3-5 Then indeed would he smash all your fine show, [*Od.* 17. 244]

18. 1-3-6 I also care about all these things, woman. But very terribly [*Il.* 6. 441]

19. 1-4-1 . . .

20. 1-4-2 speaking good things, but they were contriving evil things in their hearts. [*Od.* 17. 66]

21. 1-4-3 The glorious gifts of the gods are surely not to be cast aside, [*Il.* 3. 65]

22. 1-4-4 . . .

23. 1-4-5 . . .

24. 1-4-6 These things, Zeus—nurtured Skamander, will be as you order. [*Il.* 21. 223]

25. 1-5-1 a joy to your enemies, and a disgrace to yourself? [*Il.* 3. 51]

26. 1-5-2 Within this very year, Odysseus will arrive here, [*Od.* 14. 161; 19. 306]

27. 1-5-3 No use indeed to you, since you will not lie clad in them, [*Il.* 22. 513]

28. 1-5-4 And to the victor are to go the woman and the possessions. [*Il.* 3. 255]

29. 1-5-5 The rule of the many is no good. Let there be one ruler, [*Il.* 2. 204]

30. 1-5-6 And the gateway is full of ghosts, and full also is the courtyard, [*Od.* 20. 355]

31. 1-6-1 We have won great honor. We have killed glorious Hektor, [*Il.* 22. 393]

32. 1-6-2 Who would undertake and complete this task for? [*Il.* 10. 303]

33. 1-6-3 Not even if his gifts to me should be as numerous as the grains of sand and particles of dust, [*Il.* 9. 385]

34. 1-6-4 . . .

35. 1-6-5 . . .

36. 1-6-6 . . .

37. 2-1-1 For no island is made for driving horses or has broad meadows, [*Od.* 4. 607]

38. 2-1-2 in the past, when you were boys, did you listen to your [*Od.* 4. 688]

39. 2-1-3 . . .

40. 2-1-4 . . .

41. 2-1-5 . . .

42. 2-1-6 His gifts are hateful to me, and I honor him not a whit. [*Il.* 9. 378]

43. 2-2-1 an only beloved heir to many possessions, [*Il.* 9. 482; *Od.* 16. 19(?)]

44. 2-2-2 . . .

45. 2-2-3 . . .

46. 2-2-4 . . .

47. 2-2-5 So they thronged about him. And near [*Od.* 24. 19]

48. 2-2-6 and fashioning lies out of what nobody could see. [*Od.* 11. 366]

49. 2-3-1 be valiant, that later generations may also speak well of you. [*Od.* 1. 302]

50. 2-3-2 leaning on the grave marker over a borrow heaped up by men [*Il.* 11. 371]

51. 2-3-3 go. You have a way, and beside the sea your ships [*Il.* 9. 43]

52. 2-3-4 You will be proved a liar, and will not go on to fulfill your word. [*Il.* 19. 107]

53. 2-3-5 And his mother for her part continued the lament amid a flood of tears, [*Il.* 22. 79]

54. 2-3-6 Not even if remaining for five or six years [*Od.* 3. 115]

55. 2-4-1 So he spoke, and ordered Paion to administer a cure. [*Il.* 5. 899]

56. 2-4-2 These things, unhappy man, will I accomplish and do for you. [*Od.* 11. 80]

57. 2-4-3 How can you propose to render toil useless and ineffectual? [*Il.* 4. 26]

58. 2-4-4 a thing delayed, late of fulfillment, whose fame will never perish. [*Il.* 2. 325]

59. 2-4-5 Sooner would you grow weary and return to your native land. [*Od.* 3. 117]

60. 2-4-6 to go, that he may bring poisonous drugs from there, [*Od.* 2. 329]

61. 2-5-1 Husband, you departed from life young, and me behind as a widow [*Il.* 24. 725]

62. 2-5-2 in which way I will for sure accomplish everything and how it will be brought to pass, [*Il.* 9. 310 (?)]

63. 2-5-3 Offer me not honey-tempered wine, honored mother, [*Il.* 6. 264]

64. 2-5-4 . . .

65. 2-5-5 . . .

66. 2-5-6 Do not orphan your son and make your wife a widow. [*Il.* 6. 432]

67. 2-6-1 would that they might now eat their last and final meal here. [*Od.* 4. 685]

68. 2-6-2 It is not meet for a man who speaks in the Council to sleep all the night through, [*Il.* 2. 24]

69. 2-6-3 What's wrong with you, that you took this wrath into your heart? [*Il.* 6. 326]

70. 2-6-4 But who knows if he will one day return and punish them for their violent deeds? [*Od.* 3. 216]

71. 2-6-5 wives I will provide for both and furnish possessions [*Od.* 21. 214]

72. 2-6-6 we may try the bow and complete the contest. [*Od.* 21. 180]

73. 3-1-1 For it's no reproach to flee evil, nor by night. [*Il.* 14. 80]

74. 3-1-2 Be mindful of every form of valor. Now you needs must [*Il.* 22. 268]

75. 3-1-3 as a widow at home. And the boy is still just a baby, [*Il.* 22. 484; cf. 24. 726]

76. 3-1-4 But do you in no wise enter the moil of Ares, [*Il.* 18. 134]

77. 3-1-5 For amid misfortune mortals quickly grow old. [*Od.* 19. 360]

78. 3-1-6 . . .

79. 3-2-1 . . .

80. 3-2-2 Such a man is not alive nor will be born, [*Od.* 6. 201]

81. 3-2-3 Of a truth, child, there's nothing really wrong with this, [*Il.* 18. 128]

82. 3-2-4 Now is it no longer possible for him to find escape from us, [*Il.* 22. 219]

83. 3-2-5 we will ransom with bronze and gold, for it is within. [*Il.* 22. 50]

84. 3-2-6 drink, and do not vie with younger men. [*Od.* 21. 310]

85. 3-3-1 where are you fleeing, turning your back like a craven in the ranks? [*Il.* 8. 94]

86. 3-3-2 Would that such a man be called my husband [*Od.* 6. 244]

87. 3-3-3 plants her head in heaven and walks upon the earth. [*Il.* 4. 443]

88. 3-3-4 But Zeus does not accomplish for men all their purposes. [*Il.* 18. 328]

89. 3-3-5 and nodded for his army to survive and not to perish. [*Il.* 8. 246]

90. 3-3-6 Would that you had not pled with the noble son of Peleus, [*Il.* 9. 698]

91. 3-4-1 Honey-sweet wine has the best of you, which others also [*Od.* 21. 293]

92. 3-4-2 Act in whatever way your mind is moved, and no longer hold back. [*Il.* 22. 185]

93. 3-4-3 For it is fated for both to turn the same ground red [*Il.* 18. 329]

94. 3-4-4 keep on shooting like this, if haply you may become a light to the Danaans [*Il.* 8. 282]

95. 3-4-5 as there is no one who could keep the dogs off your head, [*Il.* 22. 348]

96. 3-4-6 You will not kill me, since I am sure not subject to Fate. [*Il.* 22. 13]

97. 3-5-1 staying right here you would help me watch over this house [*Od.* 5. 208]

98. 3-5-2 Get out of the gateway, old man, or it won't be long before you're dragged out by the foot. [*Od.* 18. 10]

99. 3-5-3 Better for a man to escape evil by flight than to be caught. [*Il.* 14. 81]

100. 3-5-4 and declare to no one, neither man nor woman, [*Od.* 13. 308]

101. 3-5-5 of wheat or barley. And the heaps fall thick and fast. [*Il.* 11. 69]

102. 3-5-6 Whatever sort of word you speak, such would you hear. [*Il.* 20. 250]

103. 3-6-1 was opposed to giving Helen to tawny Menelaos, [*Il.* 11. 125]

104. 3-6-2 or will you alter your purpose? The hearts of the good are flexible. [*Il.* 15. 203]

105. 3-6-3 Yet I for one never doubted, but at heart [*Od.* 13. 339]

106. 3-6-4 Eurymachus, it will not be so. And even you know it. [*Od.* 21. 257]

107. 3-6-5 You miserable foreigner, you have no sense at all. [*Od.* 21. 288]

108. 3-6-6 And the father granted him one thing, but denied him the other. [*Il.* 16. 250]

109. 4-1-1 Nay, go to your chambers and tend to your own work, [*Od.* 1. 356]

110. 4-1-2 Now then, do not even tell this to your wife. [*Od.* 11. 224 (alternate version)]

111. 4-1-3 would you have been stoned to death for all the wrongs you've done. [*Il.* 3. 57]

112. 4-1-4 you prayed to the immortals to see with a beard grown. [*Od.* 18. 176]

113. 4-1-5 and vow to Lycian-born Apollo the famous archer [*Il.* 4. 101]

114. 4-1-6 and no spirit of harmony unites wolves and sheep, [*Il.* 22. 263]

115. 4-2-1 Come now, let us make these concessions to one another, [*Il.* 4. 62]

116. 4-2-2 And in the throng were Strife and Uproar, and Fate—of—Death, [*Il.* 18. 535]

117. 4-2-3 . . .

118. 4-2-4 Up, rush into battle, the man you have always claimed to be. [*Il.* 4. 264]

119. 4-2-5 . . .

120. 4-2-6 You baby, what use now to keep your bow idle? [*Il.* 21. 474]

121. 4-3-1 For even fair-tressed Niobe turned her mind to food, [*Il.* 24. 602]

122. 4-3-2 after giving a mass of bronze and gold and raiment [*Od.* 5. 38]

123. 4-3-3 Surely then the journey will not be useless or fail to occur. [*Od.* 2. 273]

124. 4-3-4 One omen is best, to defend your country. [*Il.* 12. 243]

125. 4-3-5 I will gild her horns all round and sacrifice her to you. [*Il.* 10. 294]

126. 4-3-6 and you would gain every Trojan's thanks and praise, [*Il.* 4. 95]

127. 4-4-1 put in with your ship, since women are no longer trustworthy. [*Od.* 11. 456]

128. 4-4-2 It is not possible or proper to deny your request. [*Il.* 14. 212]

129. 4-4-3 would straightway fit his will to your desire and mine. [*Il.* 15. 52]

130. 4-4-4 and give him instruction. And it will be beneficial for him to obey. [*Il.* 11. 789]

131. 4-4-5 will give glory to me, and your soul to horse-famed Hades. [*Il.* 5. 654]

132. 4-4-6 fill up his ship with gold and bronze aplenty, [*Il.* 9. 137]

133. 4-5-1 but tell one part, and let the other be concealed. [*Od.* 11. 443]

134. 4-5-2 and at birth Zeus sends a weight of misery. [*Il.* 10. 71]

135. 4-5-3 alone to have intelligence, but they are flitting shades. [*Od.* 10. 495]

136. 4-5-4 yielding to his indignation. But they now withheld from him the gifts [*Il.* 9. 598]

137. 4-5-5 I rejoice at hearing what you say, son of Laërtes. [*Il.* 19. 185]

138. 4-5-6 But Zeus causes men's prowess to wax or to wane, [*Il.* 20. 242]

139. 4-6-1 a terrible man. He would be quick to blame even the blameless.

[*Il.* 11. 654]

140. 4-6-2 with all haste. For now would you capture the broad—wayed city [*Il.* 2. 66]

141. 4-6-3 Endure now, my heart. An even greater outrage did you once endure, [*Od.* 20. 18]

142. 4-6-4 You lunatic, sit still and listen to the word of others, [*Il.* 2. 200]

143. 4-6-5 had cast aside wrath and chosen friendship. [*Il.* 16. 282]

144. 4-6-6 so good it is for a son to be left by a dead [*Od.* 3. 196]

145. 5-1-1 Here then, spread under your chest a veil, [*Od.* 5. 346]

146. 5-1-2 'Tis impiety to exult over men slain. [*Od.* 22. 412]

147. 5-1-3 through immortal night, when other mortals sleep? [*Il.* 24. 363]

148. 5-1-4 How then could I forget divine Odysseus? [*Od.* 1. 65]

149. 5-1-5 lurid death and overpowering doom laid hold of [*Il.* 5. 83]

150. 5-1-6 So there's nothing else as horrible and vile as a woman [*Od.* 11. 427]

151. 5-2-1 Let us not advance to fight the Danaans around the ships. [*Il.* 12. 216]

152. 5-2-2 to put up a defense, when some fellow provokes a fight. [*Il.* 24. 369; *Od.* 16. 72; 21. 133]

153. 5-2-3 nor do children at his knees call him "papa" [*Il.* 5. 408]

154. 5-2-4 I am this very man, back home now. And after many toils [*Od.* 21. 207]

155. 5-2-5 Talk not like this. There'll be no change before [*Il.* 5. 218]

156. 5-2-6 let him stay here the while, even though he's eager for Ares. [*Il.* 19. 189]

157. 5-3-1 And do not, exulting in war and battle, [*Il.* 16. 91]

158. 5-3-2 never to have gone to bed with her and had intercourse, [*Il.* 9. 133; 19. 176]

159. 5-3-3 and moistens the lips, but fails to moisten the palate. [*Il.* 22. 495]

160. 5-3-4 Take heart! Let these matters not trouble your thoughts. [*Il.* 18. 463]

161. 5-3-5 But this mad dog I'm unable to hit. [*Il.* 8. 299]

162. 5-3-6 Keep quiet, friend, and do as I say. [*Il.* 4. 412]

163. 5-4-1 Bad deeds don't prosper. The slow man for sure overtakes the swift, [*Od.* 8. 329]

164. 5-4-2 They shut fast and locked the doors of the hall. [*Od.* 21. 236]

165. 5-4-3 Ah, poor man! Death's not at all on your mind, [*Il.* 17. 201]

166. 5-4-4 Odysseus has come and reached home, though he was long in coming. [*Od.* 23. 7]

167. 5-4-5 in full he will accomplish it at last, and the penalty they pay is great, [*Il.* 4. 161]

168. 5-4-6 and therein was Strife, and therein Valor, and therein chilling Attack, [*Il.* 5. 740]

169. 5-5-1 but 'tis most wretched to die and meet one's doom by starvation. [*Od.* 12. 342]

170. 5-5-2 shall I be laid low when I die. But good repute is now my goal, [*Il.* 18. 121]

171. 5-5-3 Up, rush into battle, the man you have always claimed to be. [*Il.*

4. 264]

172. 5-5-4 In no way do I mock you, dear child, nor am I playing tricks. [*Od.* 23. 26]

173. 5-5-5 but she stayed Alcmene's labor and stopped her from giving birth. [*Il.* 19. 119]

174. 5-5-6 But come, and hereafter I shall make amends for this, if now anything wrong [*Il.* 4. 362]

175. 5-6-1 Where are you two rushing? What causes the heart within your breast to rage? [*Il.* 8. 413]

176. 5-6-2 Pray now, let him not be too much on your mind. [*Od.* 13. 421]

177. 5-6-3 But the gods do not, I ween, give men all things at the same time. [*Il.* 4. 320]

178. 5-6-4 Talk not like this. There'll be no change before [*Il.* 5. 218]

179. 5-6-5 So he spake, but did not move the mind of Zeus by saying this. [*Il.* 12. 173]

180. 5-6-6 but Odysseus nodded no and checked him in his eagerness. [*Od.* 21. 129]

181. 6-1-1 How can you want to go alone to the ships of the Achaeans? [*Il.* 24. 203]

182. 6-1-2 him a bridegroom in his house, who left as only child a daughter [*Od.* 7. 65]

183. 6-1-3 And too, I've taken the mist from your eyes, which before was there, [*Il.* 5. 127]

184. 6-1-4 we may try the bow and complete the contest. [*Od.* 21. 180]

185. 6-1-5 And I know that my arrival was longed for by you two [*Od.* 21. 209]

186. 6-1-6 I shall dress him in a mantle and a tunic, fine garments. [*Od.* 16. 79; 17. 550; 21. 339]

187. 6-2-1 by fastening a noose sheer from a high rafter, [*Od.* 11. 278]

188. 6-2-2 remembering our excellence, of the sort that even we [*Od.* 8. 244]

189. 6-2-3 the sea's great expanse they cross, since this is the Earthshaker's gift to them. [*Od.* 7. 35]

190. 6-2-4 Nay, come on with the bow. You'll soon be sorry for obeying everybody. [*Od.* 21. 369]

191. 6-2-5 But hurry into battle, and rouse the other soldiers. [*Il.* 19. 139]

192. 6-2-6 For mighty Herakles, not even he escaped his doom, [*Il.* 18. 117]

193. 6-3-1 amends I wish to make and to give a boundless ransom. [*Il.* 9. 120; 19. 138]

194. 6-3-2 And let him stand up among the Argives and swear an oath to your [*Il.* 19. 175]

195. 6-3-3 The man is nearby. Our search will not be long, if you are willing [*Il.* 14. 110]

196. 6-3-4 and not quite suddenly, and a very god should be the cause? [*Od.* 21. 196]

197. 6-3-5 Verily, these things have already happened, and not otherwise could [*Il.* 14. 53]

198. 6-3-6 On now, follow close! In action numbers make a difference. [*Il.* 12. 412]

199. 6-4-1 surely then the gods themselves have ruined your mind. [*Il.* 7. 360; 12. 234]

200. 6-4-2 Take heart, and let your thoughts not be of death. [*Il.* 10. 383]

201. 6-4-3 by her wailing she rouse from sleep her household servants, [*Il.* 5. 413]

202. 6-4-4 Come now in strict silence, and I shall lead the way, [*Od.* 7. 30]

203. 6-4-5 are there ears for hearing, and sense and respect are dead. [*Il.* 15. 129]

204. 6-4-6 as he was growing old. But the son did not grow old in his father's armor. [*Il.* 17. 197]

205. 6-5-1 to return home and behold the day of homecoming. [*Od.* 5. 220: 8. 466]

206. 6-5-2 Apollo of the silver bow did strike the one, still sonless, [*Od.* 7. 64]

207. 6-5-3 then you may hope to see your loved ones and reach [*Od.* 7. 76]

208. 6-5-4 As for you two, I will tell you exactly how it will be. [*Od.* 21. 212]

209. 6-5-5 For so shall I proclaim, and it will be accomplished too. [*Il.* 1. 212]

210. 6-5-6 and I shall send him wherever his heart and spirit urge him. [*Od.* 16. 81; 21. 342]

211. 6-6-1 idiot? You'll soon pay when the swift hounds devour you [*Od.* 21. 363]

212. 6-6-2 You would learn what mighty hands I have to back me up. [*Od.* 20. 237; 21. 202]

213. 6-6-3 In no wise do I think he will in that event take you for himself, nor is it proper. [*Od.* 21. 322]

214. 6-6-4 here we gather, waiting day after day. [*Od.* 21. 156]

215. 6-6-5 to reach decision making secret plans. Not yet now to me [*Il.* 1.

542]

216. 6-6-6 Don't dare get it into your mind to escape from me, Dolon. [*Il.*
10. 447]

Here end the verses of the Homer oracle. May it help you!

NOTES:

Chapter 4
The Seashells of Aphrodite

Medium: Seashells, Stones, Beads, and Sand. (The reader can choose their own shells and representations.)
Method: Dropping from a cup
Mandala: Lines drawn in the sand by the querent
Mythology: None
Mode: Associations assigned to specific shells

This divination is used for relationship questions.

Crown: The querent walks on the beach searching for beauty and meaning. Look into the reflections among the pearls and shells. (Any seashell that the reader assigns to the querent.)

Pearls:

Leaf: There is life. Accept change and growth for the good it will bring.

Bead: There is introspection. Be open with reasons.

Button: There is revelry. Let the impulses carry things along.

Square: There is patience. Take time to evaluate all matters.

Spiral: There is intimacy. Let sex and romance distract for a little while.

Shells:

Spiral shaped: There are goals. Focus on your dreams.

Spike shaped: Male

Yoni shaped: Female

A man/woman is also on the beach. Seek them out for good or bad.

Plain: yes or no.

Dawn colored: The sun emerges from the ocean. Start anew, or seek the beginning.

Dusk colored: The sun sets in the ocean. Find closure or seek the end.

Orange: There is difficulty. Confront strange circumstances.

Holey White: There is aid. Welcome unexpected help from others.

Shiny: Some matters are already known. Do not take them for granted, or forget.

Dull: Some matters are unknown. Stay on guard, be ready.

Vertical Conch: There are projects, plans are in the works. Do not delay too much.

Other Mediums:

Fossil: Everyone has a past. Remember yours, or let the tide wash it away.

Crystal: There is clarity. Follow through with decisions made.

Rock: There is foundation. Steady your feet in the sand, your choices will hold.

Agate Marble: There is insight. Go with your gut feelings

Lapis Marble: There is domesticity. Be happy with the state of things.

Hematite Marble: There is need. Satisfy the desires of both parties.

NOTES:

NOTES:

Chapter 5
A Dream Cipher

Medium: Dreams
Method: Coins
Mandala: None
Mythology: Greek
Mode: Geomantic Associations

Once messages and true dreams are received, one may want to interpret it in a spiritual context. To do this, I modified the medieval system of Geomancy. In the traditions of some Arabic and African nations, a stick is used to poke random numbers of dots on the ground in four lines. Each line of dots is counted and if an even number is the final count, then two dots are chosen. If an odd number is the final count, then one dot is chosen. The end result is a figure such as this:

$$\begin{matrix} \bullet & \bullet \\ \bullet \\ \bullet \\ \bullet \end{matrix}$$

The top line resulted in an even number, while the bottom three resulted in odd numbers. In all, there are sixteen 'figures' with their own meanings. They are basic archetypes; such as boy, sadness, joy, prison, etc. They work very well with dream symbolism.

Instead of using a stick in sand or dirt, I use three coins to get even or odd numbers. If you two get or more heads, then the number is even. If you get two or more tails, then the number is odd. Any type of coin is acceptable. For each symbol, you will need four throws of the coins.

But, creating the appropriate symbols with the meaning is not enough. They need to have a context, a story to fit into. This is where the ancient Greek plays come into effect. In ancient Greece, most theatrical plays had five parts: the prologue, parados, episode, stasimon, and exodos. I have adopted these to represent the structure of a dream. For each of the five stages, the sixteen geomantic figures have different meanings. Combining both creates a 'dream cipher' used for interpretation.

Next, someone types up their dream that either has a recurring theme or is very powerful. If there is a feeling of regret, chances are the dream is a memory. If there is hope or dread, then the dream is most likely about something that will come to pass, the future. A sense of wonder or anything else is usually a reflection of the present.

The Stages

Question 1: Prologue

> Historical context: Spoken by one or two characters before the chorus appears. The prologue gave the mythological background necessary for understanding the events of the play.

> My context: Is the dream literal or figurative? Actual or symbolic? True or false?

Question 2: Parodos

> Historical context: This is the song sung by the chorus as it first enters the orchestra and dances.

> My context: Who sent the message?

Question 3: Episode

> Historical context: When the characters and chorus interact.

> My context: Is the message good or bad? Is it a warning or a reward; a blessing or a curse?

Question 4: Stasimon

> Historical context: At the end of each episode, the other characters leave the stage and the chorus dances and sings a stasimon, or choral ode. The ode usually reflects on the things said and done in the episodes and puts it into some kind of larger mythological framework.

My context: What is the message?

Question 5: Exodos

Historical context: The chorus exits singing a processional song which offers words of wisdom related to the outcome of the play.

My context: What insights does the message (dream) give?

The Associations

Populous: The Archetypes, People

1. Literal
2. Inner - Ancestors, society, friends, family (their impact on you.)
3. Good
4. The message is right in front of you, obvious.
5. Ask family for conventional wisdom, study archetypes, and symbolism.

Laetitia: The Good Memory, Joy

1. Figurative
2. Inner - the self or subconscious
3. Good
4. That good memory is guiding you at the present time.
5. How that good memory came about will help you face a difficulty now.

Tristitia: The Bad Memory, Sadness

1. Figurative

2. Inner - Your subconscious sent the message.

3. Bad

4. The main events in the dream are causing sadness.

5. Accept the sadness, ask why, or move on. Embrace or recover from the event.

Fortuna Major: The Angel, Greater Fortune

1. Literal

2. Outer - Angels

3. Good

4. The events of the dream are a message from a higher place.

5. There is help from higher beings.

Fortuna Minor: The Demon, Lesser Fortune

1. Figurative

2. Outer - Demons

3. Bad

4. The events of the dream are a warning from a dark entity.

5. There is hindrance from negative entities.

Caput Draconis: The Beginning of the Path (Destiny), Dragon's Head

1. Literal
2. Outer - The Universe
3. Good
4. You have started on your destiny.
5. The decisions you are making now will have a huge impact for a long time to come.

Cauda Draconis: The End of the Path (Destiny), Dragon's Tail

1. Literal
2. Outer - The Universe
3. Neither
4. You are close to the end of fulfilling your destiny.
5. Decisions need to be made on how you wish to end your legacy.

Via: Heaven, The Way

1. Literal
2. Outer - Heaven (or who rules there)
3. Good
4. The acts in the dream will somehow earn you a better place in your afterlife.
5. Do not dismiss minor actions, good or bad.

Carcer: Hell, Prison

1. Figurative

2. Outer - Hell (or who rules there)

3. Bad

4. The events of the dream are a warning from a dark ruler.

5. Your present course of action will lead to imprisonment.

Puella: *Inner Self* (or Childhood friend), *Girl*

If the Querent is Female:

1. Figurative

2. Inner - You

3. Neither

4. You have forgotten to do something important for yourself.

5. Revisit your past regrets and proud moments.

If the Querent is Male:

1. Either

2. If identity is known in the dream, then outer; if not, then inner.

3. Neither.

4. You have forgotten to do something important for someone else.

5. Remember past promises.

Puer: *Inner Self* **(or Childhood Friend),** *Boy*

If the Querent is Male:

1. Figurative

2. Inner - You

3. Neither

4. You have forgotten to do something important for yourself.

5. Revisit your past regrets and proud moments.

If the Querent is Female:

1. Either

2. If identity is known in the dream, then outer; if not, then inner.

3. Neither.

4. You have forgotten to do something important for someone else.

5. Remember past promises.

Acquisitio: *Eros, Gain*

1. Figurative

2. The Forces of Love or Attraction

3. Good

4. Your love for someone, or energy for your passions, is becoming powerful.

5. Be mindful of where your emotions are leading you.

Amissio: Eris, Loss

1. Literal
2. The Forces of Strife and Hate
3. Bad
4. Someone wishes to do you harm, relating to the events in the dream.
5. Ask how this enmity came about. Decide to dismiss or atone for it.

Albus: Our Realm, White

1. Figurative
2. Society, people around you in general, crowd mentality
3. Neither
4. Something you are doing is affecting your family and friends.
5. Find out what these actions are. Decide to either increase your efforts or tone them down.

Rubeus: Other Realms, Red

1. Literal
2. The Spirits (anything other than Ancestors, Demons, or Angels)
3. Good
4. Something you are doing is affecting the spirit world.
5. Find out what these actions are, and tread lightly upon the other world.

Conjunctio: Significant Other, Union

1. Literal

2. A current or possible significant other

3. Good

4. The dream is communicating the desires of the other person.

5. Decide if you want to embrace or reject those desires.

NOTES:

34

Chapter 6
The Cat's Bones

Medium: Cat Bones
Method: Throwing
Mandala: Constellation Chart (optional)
Mythology: None
Mode: Associations assigned to specific bones

The placement of the bones among certain constellations may add extra context for interpretation.

The Stone: The cat, the scout, is loyal. He/She will play among the stars for me.

The Ilium: There is movement. Recognize and harness the momentum.

The Leg: There is syzygy, these forces are linked right now. Look into the deeper meaning of this connection.

The Ribs: *If the ribs create a frame, then…* There are borders. Stay within these confines. *If the ribs do not create a frame of some kind, remove or ignore.*

Long Vertebrae: There is sight. These are things known to all.

Short Vertebrae: There is darkness. Listen to what the silence tells us, see what the shadows show us.

The Four Legs: There are elements. Seek out their balance; or draw strength from one above the rest.

Short Silver Entity: Enemies are near. Be wary.

Long Silver Entity: Allies are near. Seek their support.

Dotted Knuckle: There is love. Ride the waves and impulses of attraction.

Plain Knuckle: There is strife. Do not cause it, but harness it if it is there regardless.

Long Knuckles: There are messages. Listen.

The Sternums: There are other realms. Do not ignore their influence and their unique flow of time.

NOTES:

NOTES:

Chapter 7
Lenormand Cards

Medium: Cards
Method: Laying
Mandala: Spreads
Mythology: None
Mode: Card Meanings

The creation of the divination set is attributed to Marie Anne Lenormand.

Jokers: Chaos. Very few love chaos. Brace yourself.

(A♥) Man: One approaches. Heed his arrival.

(6♥) Stars: The stars guided the way for sailors. You can guide yourself in the same way.

(7♥) Tree: The tree stands tall, grows deep. Lean against it to ground.

(8♥) Moon: The moon is ever changing. Adapt to movement.

(9♥) Rider: The rider brings news. Recognize the urgency and listen well.

(10♥) Dog: The companion is loyal. Do not neglect him/her.

(J♥) Heart: The heart has needs. Tending to yours may also help others.

(K♥) House: One's home is their pride. Take a reprieve.

(Q♥) Stork: The stork heralds change. Do not harm the messenger.

(A♣) Ring: The ring is unending. Tend to your power.

(6♣) Cross: The cross is heavy. Bear it well.

(7♣) Mice: There are mice in the walls. Prepare for damage.

(8♣) Mountains: The mountains loom. Draw a line that cannot be crossed.

(9♣) Fox: The fox is rarely seen. Deception usually does not end well.

(10♣) Bear: The bear stands his/her ground. Decide if you are the challenger or defender.

(J♣) Whip. The whip cracks. Brace for pain.

(K♣) Clouds: The clouds darken the horizon. Allow doubt to run its course.

(Q♣) Snake: The snake bites even the snake charmer sometimes. Do not let your guard down.

(A♦) Sun: The sun rises and sets without end. Accept the inevitable.

(6♦) Clover: The four-leaf clover is lucky. Enjoy your newfound good fortune.

(7♦) Birds: The birds are chattering. Listen to see if there is anything useful being said.

(8♦) Key: Everyone has a key on them. One may open any door they wish.

(9♦) Coffin: The end has come. Say goodbye.

(10♦) Book: A good book is full of knowledge and wonders. Consult a great one.

(J♦) Scythe: The harvest comes. Wrap up any remaining matters.

(K♦) Fish: Fish sell well in the marketplace. Try out new ideas.

(Q♦) Paths: Paths lie before you. Take time to dwell, and choose wisely.

(A♠) Woman: One approaches. Heed her arrival.

(6♠) Tower: There is a tower at the center of the city. Seek out authority there.

(7♠) Letter: The letter is personal. Weigh every word.

(8♠) Garden: As is the garden, such is the gardener. Make real effort.

(9♠) Anchor: Every ship needs one. Learn how to use it.

(10♠) Ship: The ship glides on the water. Keep moving.

(J♠) Child: Children are born innocent. Ask them what they think.

(K♠) Lily: The mature lily blooms. Strive for beauty in the moment.

(Q♠) Bouquet: The bouquet is a wonderful gift. Be happy for you and the giver.

NOTES:

Chapter 8
Tarot Cards

Medium: Tarot Cards
Method: Laying
Mandala: Tarot Spreads
Mythology: Greek, Empedocles' description of the Elements
Mode: Tarot Card Meanings

Wright, M.R., *Empedocles, the Extant Fragments* (London: Bristol Classical
    Press, 1995), 164, 166-167

Optional: Can use dice for these as well.

    5: Fool
    6: Magician
    7: Empress
    Etc…

    27-30: Not meant to know, or will get no help.

Cups (Water) signify emotion and intuition. They are represented by
alchemy, mixtures, and temperance. **To Feel.**

Pentacles (Earth) signify temples, hearth and home, sacred space, and
possessions. They are represented by herbalism, offerings, and libations. **To
Collect.**

Swords (Air) signifies reason, patience, ideas, and discussion. It is
represented by ceremony, ritual, and holidays. **To Think.**

Wands (Fire) signifies passion and willpower. It is represented by spells,
workings, and divination. **To Act.**

Fire warms but also rages. Water soothes, yet crashes. The wind caresses or
roars. Earth nourishes when not trembling.

Tarot Meanings Template:

1 is the source.
2 is balancing.
3 is juggling.
4 is breaking.
5 is broken.
6 is rebuilding.
7 is assertiveness.
8 is hesitation.
9 is a leap.
10 is the completion.

Ace: It is the source of... One must give forth, seek, or share.

Two: It is the balance of... One may consider the opposite, or enjoy and add to it.

Three: It is the momentum of... One must focus.

Four: The dam is about to break in regards to... One must hold back, or surge forward.

Five: There is a crisis in regards to... Abandon these matters or accept them as they are.

Six: The pieces have been picked up about... Regroup and gather with these efforts.

Seven: Confidence shines forth in the realm of... Take new steps in this area, cultivate these actions.

Eight: Hesitation weighs down with regards to... Reconsider these types of matters.

Nine: There is not much left to do in regards to... Take a leap of faith with this subject, do not stop.

Ten: It is complete, the matters concerning... Present your results.

Page: The student has started to study... Immerse oneself into this realm, study further.

Knight: One has chosen to champion this realm. Stand fast on these matters, fight for them.

The Ruler: Make a decision

King: Liberal actions with Swords and Pentacles; conservative with Cups and Wands.

Queen: Liberal actions with Cups and Wands; conservative with Swords and Pentacles.

Ace of Swords: This is the source of patience. One must prove this ability.

Two of Swords: Listening and advising come easy. Consider opposing viewpoints.

Three of Swords: Larger problems are coming into focus. One must dwell on their own ideas.

Four of Swords: Thinking too much is causing strain. Let the plots play themselves out.

Five of Swords: No new thoughts are surfacing, scheming takes over. Find time to sit in silence, or meditate.

Six of Swords: Discarded ideas have resurfaced. Re-examine past thoughts.

Seven of Swords: One's words ring strong. Seek out new opinions.

Eight of Swords: Doubt has made its presence known. Take extra time to think before speaking.

Nine of Swords: Most angles have been considered. Take delight in counter-intuitive thinking.

Ten of Swords: Important projects have weathered much doubt. Let the results pour forth.

Page of Swords: The desire to take ideas to the next level is gaining strength. Build upon past intellectual successes.

Knight of Swords: Expertise in certain matters has been attained. Do not fear criticisms.

King of Swords: Confusion does not mean a solution is impossible. Keep seeking counsel before rendering a final judgment.

Queen of Swords: Rashness and discussion never go well together. Offer a calm voice when warranted.

Ace of Cups: This is the source of emotion. One must share their intuition.

Two of Cups: Emotional balance is always tenuous. Consider opposing feelings.

Three of Cups: There is emotional momentum. Focusing on the strongest concern would be wise.

Four of Cups: It is no longer possible to keep emotions from flooding over. Let feelings over-take for a moment.

Five of Cups: An emotional crisis has erupted. Abandon negative feelings.

Six of Cups: Relying on intuition allows the pieces to be picked up. Recover emotionally.

Seven of Cups: Personal confidence shines forth. Consider new emotional possibilities.

Eight of Cups: Hesitation halts intuitive momentum. Keep emotions in check.

Nine of Cups: There are few opportunities left for emotion or intuition. Take a leap of faith with either.

Ten of Cups: Emotional closure has been achieved. Bask in the glow, or let the issue pass.

Page of Cups: One has begun to question and examine their emotions. Seek reassurance.

Knight of Cups: Passionate choices from the past are being defended. Stand with conviction.

King of Cups: Emotional strength has been embraced. Prove this ability in front of those who question it.

Queen of Cups: There is the ability of pure emotional creativity. Take notice of those who are hurt, and help.

Ace of Wands: This is the source of fire. Feed the flames.

Two of Wands: The inner fire burns bright, but is contained. Be patient with those with little passion.

Three of Wands: Passion is building, actions grow bold. Let nothing stand in the way.

Four of Wands: Some circumstances have gotten out of control. Let passions rage.

Five of Wands: No matter the action, nothing is achieved. Halt all stubborn behaviors.

Six of Wands: The embers of passion are still warm. Rest and gather strength.

Seven of Wands: Healthy energy is present. Take on new or related causes.

Eight of Wands: Pleas have been ignored. Hold one's passion in check.

Nine of Wands: There is not much fuel left, or needed, for one's inner fire. Have trust in events put in motion.

Ten of Wands: Passion and energy have served their purposes. Enjoy the dying out of the flame.

Page of Wands: One has chosen to examine their passions and desires. Detach and observe carefully.

Knight of Wands: A choice was made to fight for related causes. Tend the fire responsibly.

King of Wands: The inner fire has never been extinguished, and now rages. Focus even more on personal causes.

Queen of Wands: Passionate decisions have been made without question. Respond with a light hand when provoked.

Ace of Pentacles: This represents one's most sacred space. Learn how to share it with others if preferred.

Two of Pentacles: The temple is not cluttered, there is no hoarding. Add to or take away from the sacred space and possession.

Three of Pentacles: One is building. Let nothing distract.

Four of Pentacles: The house of cards is about to fall. Try all last measures.

Five of Pentacles: The temple has fallen, possessions have lost sentimental value. Let the pieces lay as they are.

Six of Pentacles: It is possible to rebuild. Make efforts and pick up the pieces, new and old are interchangeable.

Seven of Pentacles: The temple is now even more sacred. Make its possessions more powerful.

Eight of Pentacles: Even in a temple, there can be distractions. Wait for them to pass.

Nine of Pentacles: The last thing added is always the most comfortable. Try new decorations and let the objects place themselves.

Ten of Pentacles: The temple stands tall, all that is wished for is acquired. Bless all that is important.

Page of Pentacles: The temple shines, it is time to study there. Put all the best things on the altar.

Knight of Pentacles: One is proud of their space. Defend it at all costs.

King of Pentacles: In front of the hearth is the best place to find rest. Find the stillness in the temple.

Queen of Pentacles: Comfort and peace at home have never been taken for granted. Re-consecrate the sacred space if so desired.

0. The Fool is purposefully lost. Keep wandering.

I. The Magician has mastered the elements. Work magic.

II. The High Priestess controls her domain. Nurture all those in it.

III. The Empress is obeyed. Rule wisely.

IV. The Emperor observes. Rule strongly.

V. The Hierophant has seen much. Pass along wisdom.

VI. The Lovers enjoy each other's presence. Conjoin at all levels of being.

VII. The Chariot has journeyed swiftly but safely. Arrive, or announce your presence.

VIII. Justice has considered all options. Dispense a ruling.

IX. The Hermit ponders. Retreat into solitude.

X. The Wheel has always turned. Take a chance.

XI. Strength is not brute force. Stand firm with conviction.

XII. The Hanged Man sways. Wait for a solution to present itself.

XIII. Death comes for all. Enjoy the transformation.

XIV. Temperance delights in mixtures. Yield to others as well as yourself.

XV. The Devil will always want more. Plot or scheme, if appropriate.

XVI. The Tower does not have strong foundations. Fall apart or give up.

XVII. The Star is eternal. Take comfort in its guiding.

XVIII. The Moon is fluid in its movements. Hide oneself if there is cause.

XIX. The Sun is ever present. Reveal your soul in all its glory.

XX. Judgment awaits us all. Decide how it will be faced.

XXI. The World is infinite. Embrace wonder and seek awe whenever possible.

NOTES:

NOTES:

Chapter 9
A Promethean Oracle Deck

Medium: Cards (A full deck was not used.)
Method: Laying
Mandala: Spreads
Mythology: None
Mode: Card Meanings

Ace of Hearts: You are not connected. Lean against an old tree; ground and recharge.

Three of Hearts: There is struggle. Be like a duck in water.

Four of Hearts: There is a wound. Seek out a spiritual healer.

Seven of Hearts: The shadows are active. Consult a haunted doll.

Eight of Hearts: A new skill is needed. Learn one.

Nine of Hearts: An Angel is active. Ask why.

Ten of Hearts: There is a situation that requires a divination. Choose which one to do.

Jack of Hearts: A divination would not be useful. Do not do one.

Ace of Clubs: There is a door nearby. Pay attention to your surroundings.

Two of Clubs: The left-hand path will be better. Take it.

Three of Clubs: Your garnet influences are needed. Harness strength, knowledge, and wisdom.

Four of Clubs: There was an echo. Find out who sent it and what the message was.

Five of Clubs: The answer lies in dreams. Rely more on your dream power.

Seven of Clubs: Something or someone is coming. Conceal yourself among the trees and listen.

Eight of Clubs: You have much to offer. Look for opportunities to teach.

Nine of Clubs: The well has run dry. Find a way to fill it.

Ten of Clubs: You are not supposed to know. Let the issue pass.

Queen of Clubs: A different set of thoughts is needed. Consult your Spirit Guide.

Ace of Diamonds: There is nothing here. Move on.

Two of Diamonds: In the here and now, the correct path was chosen. Do not deviate.

Three of Diamonds: In the here and now, the incorrect path was chosen. Reconsider past actions and decisions.

Four of Diamonds: The Elements are out of balance, a different aspect is needed. Consult the Holy Mind.

Five of Diamonds: A hawk is flying above, surveying. Take a larger look.

Seven of Diamonds: There is too much to know. Find a distraction.

Nine of Diamonds: Movement is needed. Travel, walk, etc.

Ten of Diamonds: You already know the answer. Take a deep breath and understand the situation.

Jack of Diamonds: Inspiration lies among the stones. Consult your gems.

King of Diamonds: Inspiration lies among your books. Read a good myth.

Queen of Diamonds: Inspiration lies among your skulls. Consult your companions.

Ace of Spades: Death is close. Steel yourself, compose.

Two of Spades: The right-hand path will be better. Take it.

Nine of Spades: A Demon is active. Ask why.

Ten of Spades: There is a situation that requires magic. Use it.

Jack of Spades: Magic here would not be useful. Do not use it.

Jokers: The fools have the scepter. Do not engage or encourage; do nothing.

The Sixes: Time

Six of Diamonds: There are things in this time that need addressing. Stay the course, focus here and now.

Six of Hearts: There are things in dream time that need addressing. Do dream magic, create dreams.

Six of Clubs: There are things that need addressing in royal (generational) time. Seek out or make decrees.

Six of Spades: There are things in afterlife time that need addressing. Speak to or with the dead and ancestors.

NOTES:

NOTES:

Chapter 10
Omens and Echoes

Medium: Wood coins, or anything that can be engraved
Method: Pulling blind out of a bag
Mandala: None
Mythology: Greek
Mode: Deity names and associations, yes/no stanzas

Many cultures have a myth about a deity showing its true presence to a mortal and causing pain or death to that mortal with its divine glory. These stories show that the Gods cannot show us their true forms. This system is for hearing the echoes, the whispers, of whatever deity a person prays to. This is only one method for doing it, you can use the pantheon of your choice with their associations.

We used an oak branch one inch thick and cut off pieces that are coin size. You could use any other type of wood or clay. You might consider making the deity coins a different size from the number coins. They will be easier to tell apart if they are all in one bag. On one set, engrave the names of the proper deities on one or both sides. On another set engrave the number of yes/no stanzas on one side only. The coins can be kept in a bag. If an omen is received or an oracle is desired, draw out a coin with a name and a coin with a number. The named coin is the deity that sent the message. The number coin is the message sent, depending on the heads or tails designation. The negative answer is tails. The number 7 coin can be flipped like a quarter if you have a simple yes/no question or if you need clarification.

Deities

Aphrodite (Αφροδιτη): love, physical pleasures, relationships

Apollo (Απολλων): male realm, music, art

Ares (Αρης): war, aggression, defense

Artemis (Αρτεμις): female realm, hunting, childbirth

Athena (Αθηνη): wisdom, civil judgement

Demeter (Δημητηρ): agriculture, herbalism, seasons

Dionysus (Διονυσος): wine, revelry, holidays

Hades (Ἁιδης): death, ghosts, underworld

Hecate (Εκατη): shadows, unknown

Hephaestus (Ἡφαιστος): fire, trade skills

Hera (Ἡρη): royal wife, marriage

Hestia (Εστια): hearth, passion, domesticity

Persephone (Περσεφονη): Spring, life, unwilling participation

Poseidon (Ποσειδων): the sea, rivers, horses

Prometheus (Προμηθευς): divine knowledge, divine assistance

Zeus (Ζευς): royal husband, divine law, fate

Yes/No Stanzas

1. You are on the right/wrong path.
2. There is something to remember/forget.
3. Death is in front/behind.
4. You are in the dark/light.
5. You do/don't know.
6. The gods are/aren't with you.
7. You are right/wrong.
8. You are/aren't the aggressor.
9. There is/isn't a connection to something deeper.
10. The door is/isn't open.
11. You are/aren't lost.

12. Do/Do not use magic.

13. You are/aren't alone.

14. You are/aren't ready for the next step.

15. You should/shouldn't seek sacred space.

16. You should/shouldn't do more divination.

17. The entities are/aren't listening.

18. There are/aren't other types of energy involved.

19. This issue is/isn't about you.

20. You do/don't need assistance from others.

21. There is an issue that needs resolved/abandoned.

NOTES:

Chapter 11
Runes

Medium: Stones or Sticks
Method: Drawing like lots
Mandala: Optional
Mythology: Norse
Mode: Edda Stanzas

Bellows, Henry Adams, *The Poetic Edda* (Princeton University Press, 1936), https://books.google.com/books?id=oQjLIWSShrcC&printsec=front cover#v=onepage&q&f=false, Last accessed on November 17, 2018.

Byock, Jesse, *The Prose Edda* (New York: Penguin Classics, 2005)

Byock, Jesse, *The Saga of the Volsungs, The Norse Epic of Sigurd the Dragon Slayer* (New York: Penguin Classics, 1999)

Dickens, Bruce, *Runic and Heroic Poems of the Old Teutonic Peoples* (London: Cambridge University Press, 1915)

Larrington, Carolyne, *The Poetic Edda* (Oxford: Oxford University Press, 1996)

MacLeod, Mindy and Bernard Mees, *Runic Amulets and Magic Objects* (Woodbridge: The Boydell Press, 2006), 14

The goal of this chapter was to take the rune descriptions from the stanzas of the Larrington's <u>Sayings of the High One</u> and match them up to the proper runes and their names from the table in MacLeod's and Mees' *Runic Amulets and Magic Objects*. Other sources were used to give supporting evidence to my findings. Using all of that information, I created divination oracles to accompany stanza and rune symbol. Conjecture was used for the rune 'Estate'. This is a starting point, and it is my hope that scholars will note the process and match the stanzas up more accurately. For magical purposes, follow the oracle with the phrase: "I cast this rune to bring about/cause...etc."

The Old English, Nordic, and Gothic names and symbols were all taken from the table on page 14 of MacLeod's *Runic Amulets and Magic Objects*.

ᚹ

Old English: joy. Nordic: (blank). Gothic: joy.

Oracle: Joy makes the sun and moon shine brighter. Summon the courage to share this experience.

<u>Sayings of the High One</u>, Larrington, pgs. 15-38
Stanza 146
> "I know those spells which a ruler's wife doesn't know,
> Nor any man's son;
> 'Help' one is called,
> And that will help you
> Against accusations and sorrows
> And every sort of anxiety."

<u>The Anglo-Saxon Runic Poem</u>, Dickens, pgs. 12-23
Lines 22-24
> "W. (bliss) ...he enjoys who knows not suffering, sorrow nor anxiety, and has prosperity and happiness and a good enough house."

ᚠ

Old English: torch. Nordic: ulcer, sore. Gothic: boil.

All need healing, high and low. Write the rune of sickness on a tree so that it may transfer to the bark.

Sayings of the High One, Larrington, pgs. 15-38
Stanza 147
> "I know a second one which the sons of men need,
> Those who want to live as physicians."

Lay of Sigrdrifa, Larrington, pgs. 166-173
Stanza 9
> "Helping-runes you must know if you want to assist
> And release children from women;
> They shall be cut on the palms and clasped on the joints,
> And then the *disir* asked for help."

Stanza 11
> "Limb-runes you must know if you want to be a healer
> And know how to see to wounds;
> On the bark they must be cut and of the tree of the wood,
> On those whose branches bend east."

Lay of Sigrdrifa, Bellows, Translation note:
> "10. Branch-runes: runes cut in the bark of trees. Such runes were believed to transfer sickness from the invalid to the tree. Some editors, however, have changed "limrunar" ("branch runes") to "lifrunar" ("life-runes")."

ᚠ

Old English: mouth. Nordic: river-mouth, As, god. Gothic: ?

No one looks kindly on those who carry chains for others. Be careful of bonds that are placed hastily.

<u>Sayings of the High One</u>, Larrington, pgs. 15-38
Stanza 148
> "I know a third one which is very useful to me,
> Which fetters my enemy;
> The edges of my foes I can blunt,
> Neither weapon nor club will bite for them."

<u>Loki's Quarrel</u>, Larrington, pgs. 84-96
Stanza 41
> "Freyr said:
> A wolf I see there lying before a river mouth,
> Until the gods are torn asunder;
> Thus you shall be bound - unless you are now silent -
> Next, maker of harm!"

<u>Lay of Sigrdrifa</u>, Bellows, Translation note:
> "41. The mouth of the river: according to Snorri, the chained Fenrir "roars horribly, and the slaver runs from his mouth, and makes the river called Vam; he lies there till the doom of the gods." "

ᛝ

Old English: Ing. Nordic: (blank). Gothic: Ing.

There are many trapped in chains. Find a way to break the bonds.

Sayings of the High One, Larrington, pgs. 15-38
Stanza 149
> "I know a fourth one if men put
> Chains upon my limbs;
> I can chant so that I can walk away,
> Fetters spring from my feet,
> And bonds from my hands."

Loki's Quarrel, Larrington, pgs. 84-96
Stanza 37
> "Tyr said:
> Freyr is the best of all the bold riders
> In the courts of the Æsir;
> He makes no girl cry nor any man's wife,
> And looses each man from captivity."

I

Old English: ice. Nordic: ice. Gothic: ice.

The happenings of the world can be like a raging waterfall. Seek out a still reflection.

Sayings of the High One, Larrington, pgs. 15-38
Stanza 150
> "I know a fifth if I see, shot in malice,
> A dart flying amid the army:
> It cannot fly so fast that I cannot stop it
> If I see it with my eyes."

The Anglo-Saxon Runic Poem, Dickens, pgs. 12-23
Lines 29-31
> "I. (ice) is very cold and immeasurably slippery; it glistens as clear as glass and most like to gems; it is a floor wrought by the frost, fair to look upon."

†

Old English: need. Nordic: constraint. Gothic: ?

There is a poison present. Constrain yourself to only necessary actions.

<u>Sayings of the High One</u>, Larrington, pgs. 15-38
Stanza 151
> "I know a sixth one if a man wounds me
> With roots of the sap-filled wood: (herb)
> And that man who conjured to harm me,
> The evil consumes him, not me."

<u>Lay of Sigrdrifa</u>, Larrington, pgs. 166-173
Stanza 7
> "Ale-runes must you know if you do not want another's wife
> To beguile your trust, if you believe her;
> On a horn they should be cut and on the back of the hand,
> And mark your nail with "Naud." "

Stanza 8
> "The cup should be signed over and guarded against mischief,
> And garlic thrown in the liquid:
> Though I know that for you there will never be
> Mead blended with malice."

<u>Concerning the Volsungs</u>, Byock, *The Saga of the Volsungs*, pg. 51
> "She came a third time and told him to drain the horn if he had the
> courage of the Volsungs. Sinfjotli the horn and said: 'This drink has
> been poisoned.' 'Strain it through your mustache, my son,' Sigmund in
> reply. The king was very drunk at the time, and that is why he spoke as
> he did. Sinfjotli drank and immediately collapsed."

H

Old English: hail. Nordic: hail. Gothic: hail.

Fire consumes all. Call to the sky for relief.

<u>Sayings of the High One</u>, Larrington, pgs. 15-38
Stanza 152
> "I know a seventh one if I see towering flames
> In the hall about my companions:
> It can't burn so widely that I can't counteract it,
> I know the spells to chant."

<u>The Anglo-Saxon Runic Poem</u>, Dickens, pgs. 12-23
Lines 25-26
> "H. (hail) is the whitest of grain; it is whirled from the vault of heaven
> and is tossed about by gusts of wind and then it melts into water."

X

Old English: gift. Nordic: (blank). Gothic: gift.

Enmity is brewing. Seek or give a gift.

<u>Sayings of the High One</u>, Larrington, pgs. 15-38
Stanza 153
> "I know an eighth one, which is most useful
> For everyone to know;
> Where hatred flares up between the sons of warriors,
> Then I can quickly bring settlement."

Stanza 41
> "With weapons and gifts friends should gladden one another,
> That is most obvious;
> Mutual givers and receivers are friends for longest,
> If the friendship is going to work at all."

<u>Lay of Sigrdrifa</u>, Larrington, pgs. 166-173
Stanza 12
> "Speech-runes you must know if you want no one to
> Repay sorrow with enmity;
> Wind them about, weave them about,
> Set them all together
> At that meeting where people must go
> To fully constituted courts."

ᚢ

Old English: aurochs. Nordic: drizzle, aurochs. Gothic: aurochs.

The waves are crashing. Seek safe harbor.

Sayings of the High One, Larrington, pgs. 15-38
Stanza 154
    "I know a ninth one if I am in need,
    If I must protect my ship at sea;
    The wind I can lull upon the wave
    And quieten all the sea to sleep."

Lay of Sigrdrifa, Larrington, pgs. 166-173
Stanza 10
    "Sea-runes you must cut if you want to have guaranteed
    The sail-horses on the sea;
    On the prow they must be cut and on the rudder,
    And burnt into the oar with fire;
    However steep the breakers or dark the waves, yet you'll come safe
    from the sea."

The Icelandic Runic Poem, Dickens, pgs. 28-33
Stanza 2
    "Shower = lamentation of the clouds, and ruin of the hay-harvest, and
    abomination of the shepherd."

First Poem of Helgi Hundingsbani, Larrington, pgs. 114-122
Stanza 29
    "Heldi ordered the high sail to be set,
    His crew did not fail at the meeting of the waves,
    When Aegir's terrible daughter
    Wanted to capsize the stay-bridled wave-horse."

ᛗ

Old English: horse. Nordic: (blank). Gothic: horse.

Someone is causing harm and sowing chaos. Toss a stick into the spokes of an antagonizer.

Sayings of the High One, Larrington, pgs. 15-38
Stanza 155
> "I know a tenth one if I see witches
> playing up in the air;
> I can bring it about that they can't make their way back
> To their own shapes, their own spirits."

Gylfaginning, Byock, *The Prose Edda*, pg. 43
> "The fourteenth is Gna. Frigg sends her to different worlds on errands. She has the horse named Hofvarpnir [Hoof Kicker], which rides through the air and on the sea. Once some Vanir saw her path as she rode through the air, and one of them said: "What flies there? What fares there or moves through the air?" She replied: "I fly not though I fare and move through the air on Hofvarpnir, the one whom Hamskerpir got with Gardrofa."
>
> From Gna's name comes the custom of saying that something gnaefer [looms] when it rises up high."

ᛋ

Old English: sun. Nordic: sun. Gothic: sun.

Those who lead shine the brightest. Do not neglect the safety of all involved.

Sayings of the High One, Larrington, pgs. 15-38
Stanza 156
    "I know an eleventh if I have to lead
    Loyal friends into battle;
    Under the shield I chant, and they journey inviolate,
    Safely to the battle, safely from the battle
    Safely they come everywhere."

Lay of Sigrdrifa, Larrington, pgs. 166-173
Stanza 15
    "On a shield they should be cut,
    The one which stands before the shining god,
    On the ears of Arvak and the hoof of Alsvinn..."

Grimnir's Sayings, Larrington, pgs. 50-60
Stanza 37
    "Arvak and Alsvid, they must pull wearily
    The sun from here;
    And under their saddle-bows the cheerful gods,
    The Æsir, have hidden iron bellows."

Stanza 38
    "Svalin is the name of a shield which stands before the sun,
    Before the shining god;
    Mountain and sea I know would burn up
    If it fell away from the front."

ᚱ

Old English: ride. Nordic: ride. Gothic: ride.

One who knows death has traveled. Do not be irresponsible with this knowledge.

Sayings of the High One, Larrington, pgs. 15-38
Stanza 157

> "I know a twelfth one if I see, up in a tree,
> A dangling corpse in a noose:
> I can so carve and colour the runes
> That the man walks and talks with me."

Baldr's Dreams, Larrington, pgs. 243-245
Stanza 2

> "Up rose Odin, the sacrifice for men,
> And on Sleipnir he laid a saddle;
> Down he rode to Mist-hell,
> There he met a dog coming from hell."

Stanza 4

> "Then Odin rode by the eastern doors,
> Where he knows the seeress's grave to be;
> He began to speak a corpse-reviving spell for the wise woman,
> Until reluctantly she rose, spoke these corpse-words:"

Stanza 5

> " 'Which man is that, unknown to me,
> who is making me travel this difficult road?
> I was snowed upon, I was rained upon,
> Dew fell upon me, dead I've been for a long time.' "

↑

Old English: Tyr, glory. Nordic: Tyr, god. Gothic: god.

Even the strong seek blessings from others. Be gracious and humble if one asks for guidance.

Sayings of the High One, Larrington, pgs. 15-38
Stanza 158
 "I know a thirteenth if I shall pour water
 Over a young warrior:
 He will not fall though he goes into battle,
 Before swords he will not sink."

Lay of Sigrdrifa, Larrington, pgs. 166-173
Stanza 6
 "Victory-runes you must cut if you want to have victory,
 And cut them on your sword hilt;
 Some on the blade-guards, some on the plates,
 And invoke Tyr twice."

Old English: year. Nordic: year. Gothic: year.

Sometimes wisdom resides in memory. Call forth a remembrance that evokes power.

Sayings of the High One, Larrington, pgs. 15-38
Stanza 159
> "I know a fourteenth if I have to reckon up
> The gods before men:
> Æsir and elves, I know the difference between them,
> Few who are not wise know that."

Lay of Sigrdrifa, Larrington, pgs. 166-173
Note between Stanzas 2 and 3
> "Sigurd sat down and asked her name. She took a horn full of mead and gave him a memory-drink."

Stanza 6
> "Beer I give you, apple-tree of battle,
> Mixed with magical power and mighty glory;
> It is full of spells and favourable letters,
> Good charms and joyful runes."

Song of Hyndla, Larrington, pgs. 253-259
Stanza 45
> "Give some memory-ale to my boar,
> So that he can hold fast to all these words
> From this conversation on the third morning,
> When he and Angantyr reckon up their lineage."

ᛏ

Old English: grave. Nordic: (blank). Gothic: (blank).

There are rumblings from deep within the earth. Listen with a wise ear, seek counsel if need be.

<u>Sayings of the High One</u>, Larrington, pgs. 15-38
Stanza 160

>"I know a fifteenth, which the dwarf Thiodrerir
>Chanted before Delling's doors:
>Powerful he sang for the Æsir and before the elves,
>Wisdom to Sage."

<u>Seeress' Prophecy</u>, Larrington, pgs. 3-13
Stanza 48

>"What of the Æsir? What of the elves?
>All Giantland groans. The Æsir are in council.
>The dwarfs howl before their rocky doors,
>The princes of the mountain wall -
>Do you understand yet, or what more?"

<u>Svipdagsmol</u>, Bellows, Translation:
Stanza 15

>"Now fare on the way, where danger waits,
>Let evils not lessen thy love!
>I have stood at the door, of the earth-fixed stones,
>The while I chanted thee charms."

ᛒ

Old English: birch. Nordic: birch twig. Gothic: birch twig.

Free will is a gift from the Gods. Do not infringe upon others' if you do not wish to lose your own.

Sayings of the High One, Larrington, pgs. 15-38
Stanza 161

> "I know a sixteenth if I want to have all
> A clever woman's heart and love-play:
> I can turn the thoughts of the white-armed woman
> And change her mind entirely."

Skirnir's Journey, Larrington, pgs. 61-68
Stanza 6

> "Freyr said:
> In the courts of Gymir I saw walking
> A girl pleasing to me.
> Her arms shine and from there
> All the sea and air catch light."

Stanza 26

> "Skirnir said:
> I strike you with a taming wand, and I will take you,
> Girl, to my desires;
> There you shall go where the sons of men
> Shall never see you again."

Stanza 32

> "I went to the forest, to the living wood,
> To get a potent branch;
> A potent branch I got."

ᛟ

Old English: land. Norgic: (blank). Gothic: inheritance.

Possessions only turn a shallow eye. Be wary of those casting about coins, seek a warm fire instead.

Sayings of the High One, Larrington, pgs. 15-38
Stanza 162

    "I know a seventeenth, so that scarcely any
    Young girl will want to shun me.
    Of these spells, Loddfafnir,
    You will long be in want;
    Though they'd be good for you, if you got them,
    Useful if you learned them,
    Handy, if you had them."

ᚱ

Old English: liquid. Nordic: liquid. Gothic: liquid.

Wisdom is the true nourisher of life. Raise a chalice to oneself and the Gods if one seeks it.

<u>Sayings of the High One</u>, Larrington, pgs. 15-38
Stanza 163
> "I know an eighteenth, which I shall never teach
> To any girl or any man's wife -
> It's always better when just one person knows,
> That follows at the end of the spells -
> Except that one woman whom my arms embrace,
> Or who may be my sister."

<u>Lay of Sigrdrifa</u>, Larrington, pgs. 166-173
Stanza 13
> "Mind-runes you must know if you want to be
> Wiser in spirit than every other man;
> Hropt interpreted them,
> Cut them, thought them out,
> From that liquid which had leaked
> From the skull of Heiddraupnir
> And from Hoddrofnir's horn."

<u>Gylfaginning</u>, Byock, *The Prose Edda*, pg. 24
> "Under the root that goes to the frost giants is the Well of Mimir. Wisdom and intelligence are hidden there, and Mimir is the name of the well's owner. He is full of wisdom because he drinks of the well from the Gjallarhorn. All-Father went there and asked for one drink from the well, but he did not get this until he gave one of his eyes as a pledge. As it says in the Sibyl's Prophecy..."

Summary of the Oracles

ᛈ Joy makes the sun and moon shine brighter. Summon the courage to share this experience.

ᛘ All need healing, high and low. Write the rune of sickness on a tree so that it may transfer to the bark.

ᚠ No one looks kindly on those who carry chains for others. Be careful of bonds that are placed hastily.

ᛉ There are many trapped in chains. Find a way to break the bonds.

ᛁ The happenings of the world can be like a raging waterfall. Seek out a still reflection.

ᛏ There is a poison present. Constrain yourself to only necessary actions.

ᚼ Fire consumes all. Call to the sky for relief.

ᚷ Enmity is brewing. Seek or give a gift.

ᚿ The waves are crashing. Seek safe harbor.

ᛗ Someone is causing harm and sowing chaos. Toss a stick into the spokes of an antagonizer.

ᛄ Those who lead shine the brightest. Do not neglect the safety of all involved.

ᚱ One who knows death has traveled. Do not be irresponsible with this knowledge.

↑ Even the strong seek blessings from others. Be gracious and humble if one asks for guidance.

ᛋ Sometimes wisdom resides in memory. Call forth a remembrance that evokes power.

ᛏ There are rumblings from deep within the earth. Listen with a wise ear, seek counsel if need be.

ᛒ Free will is a gift from the Gods. Do not infringe upon others' if you do not wish to lose your own.

ᛦ Possessions only turn a shallow eye. Be wary of those casting about coins, seek a warm fire instead.

ᚠ Wisdom is the true nourisher of life. Raise a chalice to oneself and the Gods if one seeks it.

NOTES:

NOTES:

NOTES:

Chapter 12
Astrology

Medium: The Planets, Elements, and Moons
Method: The Orbits
Mandala: The Constellation Borders
Mythology: Greek
Mode of Communication: Oracles and Interactions

The Planets associations are Design, Love, Life, Strife, Royalty, Afterlife, Dreams, Depths

The Constellations associations are Legacy Relic, Divine Power, Immortal Bond, Great Resolve, Challenging Strength, Tempered Wisdom, Justice and Movement, Power and Purpose, Healing and Limits, Forest Solitude, Dauntless cleverness, Destinies, and Love versus Chaos.

The Planets

☿: Mercury brings design, keeping the heavens organized. One can shape anything they wish.

♀: Venus brings love. The forces of attraction should not be taken lightly.

♁: Earth brings life. Find the sacredness in everything.

♂: Mars brings strife. The forces of discord should not be ignored.

♃: Jupiter rules our realm. One can ponder all and make a decree in his honor.

♄: Saturn rules death and the afterlife with the ancients, ancestors, and elders. No one can avoid this realm or its knowledge.

♅: Uranus rules dreams and the realm of the Oneiroi. Seek out many wonders from him.

♆: Neptune rules the deep. The darkness calls out to be embraced, approach the boundaries with resolve.

The Mandala

♈ Aries: The Fleece hangs in the grove. There is a powerful and sought-after legacy. (Fire)

♉ Taurus: The Bull charges with glistening horns. Divine power manifests on earth. (Earth)

♊ Gemini: The Twins share their time among the stars. An immortal bond can raise one to the heavens. (Air)

♋ Cancer: The Crab approaches without hesitation. Great resolve is found in even the smallest beings. (Water)

♌ Leo: The Lion leaps at its rival. There is always something stronger. (Fire)

♍ Virgo: The Virgin observes all those that stand before her. All actions are tempered with wisdom. (Earth)

♎ Libra: The Scales sway with the weight of truth. Laws and morals must be flexible, a scale can move. (Air)

♏ Scorpius: The Scorpion strikes at its prey. Power needs a purpose. (Water)

⛎ Ophiuchus: The Great Physician is struck down. A healer must know their limits. (Earth)

♐ Sagittarius: The Archer aims through the trees. There are those who find solace in the forests. (Fire)

♑ Capricornus: The Aegipan assists in victory. Cleverness defeats fear. (Earth)

♒ Aquarius: The Cupbearer serves the King of the Gods. Divinities give destinies. (Air)

♓ Pisces: The Mother and Son take refuge from the battle. The bonds of love can withstand any chaos. (Water)

Planets with Constellations

☿: Mercury - Design and Shaping

1: ☿ ♈ There is a crafted item that can aid destinies, an ancestral heirloom. Help with the legacies of others, but resist letting doubt influence design.

2: ☿ ♉ The influences of the Muses is strong. Be more receptive to the forces of harmony.

3: ☿ ♊ Bonding comes with the greatest of ease. Take pride in the building and shaping of strong relationships.

4: ☿ ♋ There is a proven patience. Thrive on creating monumental tasks.

5: ☿ ♌ One enjoys challenges when new regimens present themselves. Find unique ways to recognize your own strengths.

6: ☿ ♍ The influence of arbitration is available. Test out the boundaries of what it means to be patient.

7: ☿♎ Design sheds light on truth, one is a mandala creator. Be creative when justice is administered.

8: ☿♏ A ruler channels energy into things that affect others. Take down old barriers, set new ones.

9: ☿♅ Design influences healing. Be a resourceful gatherer and enjoy new healing discoveries.

10: ☿♐ Divine pathfinding has been gifted. Recognize that a sacred grove is always at hand.

11: ☿♑ A trickster lies within, and it will take much to be outwitted. Be mindful of good or bad intentions.

12: ☿♒ There is the ability to create destinies for those without one, to set the lost back on a path. Take great care with this responsibility.

13: ☿♓ One can create jewels. Abandon bonds with those who do not desire jewels made for them, find those that do.

♀: Venus - Love

14: ♀♈ A divine partner is on the periphery one prefers a companion on the journey. Be more attentive than usual to the feelings of others.

15: ♀♉ Attraction manifests through divine power. Search for gifts that can cause great joy or pain.

16: ♀♊ Immense joy follows when a strong bond forms, soulmates are near. Take heed of one's emotional power over others.

17: ♀ ♋ Sacrifice comes easy, martyrdom does not. Do not surrender unless there is confidence that real love is present.

18: ♀ ♌ Love influences strength. Take risks, be assertive with desired relationships.

19: ♀ ♍ One is accomplished at nurturing. Enjoy success in parenting, teaching, or mentorship.

20: ♀ ♎ Companionship blossoms during an adventure. Do not feel ashamed for always wanting to travel with another.

21: ♀ ♏ It is quite easy to be the savior of relationships. Learn from this skill, teach others as well.

22: ♀ ♅ There are burns and scars from past relationships. Remember how healing did come in the end.

23: ♀ ♐ An unusual sense of oneness with all things is achieved. Ignore any feelings of isolation, for they are not real.

24: ♀ ♑ One is well seasoned in the matters of love. Make sure standards are clear if set higher than normal.

25: ♀ ♒ The demeanor of a royal consort emanates. Enjoy setting a good example.

26: ♀ ♓ Love and attraction confront chaos. Be very aware of one's own tremendous selfless power.

27: ♂ ♈ Life follows this wanderer. Be sure to replenish energy when spent.

28: ♂ ♉ Unique spiritual skills have developed. Use them before the opportunity in this life passes.

29: ♂ ♊ The ability for strong empathy can overwhelm one at times. Learn how to ease these moments.

30: ♂ ♋ Misguided optimism can be blinding. Be sure to focus before lending time and energy to others.

31: ♂ ♌ The desire to be physically active is powerful. One finds strength sacred, seek out a sleeping lion.

32: ♂ ♍ An unusually old soul is present. Be joyous, remember why you came back.

33: ♂ ♎ One has the skill to cross others through terrifying gateways. Comfort those who are being escorted.

34: ♂ ♏ The desire for clear goals and discipline is strong. Only apply these standards to others if they ask.

35: ♂ ♅ One has been healed, and this energy is contagious. Do not let just anyone bask in this but give much when it does happen.

36: ♂ ♐ Solitude is much desired, but even a hermit should be hospitable. Be gracious to guests, for one never knows who they are.

37: ♂ ♑ There is a tendency to be a resourceful and a good mate. Seek out another like you, the power shared will be worth the effort.

38: ♄♒ One has chosen to undertake a divine errand. Be aware of the task, but do not let it consume daily life.

39: ♄♓ Victories come easy, one may lend energy to others so they can also achieve victories. Balance out the feelings of success and vindication.

♂: Mars - Strife

40: ♂♈ There is skill at enduring the last remnants of effort. Remember that what is lost may be gone forever.

41: ♂♉ A curse is present. Learn why it was cast and dispel it.

42: ♂♊ Many ties were severed. Decide if one's own fiery qualities should be passed on to others.

43: ♂♋ There is an accepted punishment. Bear it with grace or unshackle the soul.

44: ♂♌ The choice was made to have no limits, no regrets. Know that there will be great chaos when an equal arrives, but it need not be destructive.

45: ♂♍ Foolishness can be a delight to some. Choose these times carefully.

46: ♂♎ Anarchist tendencies come naturally. Decide if they are to be used for the greater good or not.

47: ♂♏ There must always be a hangman, an executioner, for Death works not alone. Do not let knowledge of the end of things extinguish the spirit too early.

48: ♂ ♅ Disease is present. Be healed or be stronger.

49: ♂ ♐ There are some who enjoy decay and entropy. Allow these skills to be a boon when needed.

50: ♂ ♑ Wickedness is like a golden thorn, admired for its beauty when not in use. Enjoy these golden thorns as decorations, they prick all when in use.

51: ♂ ♒ One delights in being an antagonist. Seek out a worthy protagonist.

52: ♂ ♓ The family narrowly escaped the battle. Do not return before the war is over, a stalemate may still be in effect.

♃: Jupiter - Royalty

53: ♃ ♈ One has inherited a coat of arms, a clan reputation. Bask in its glory, do not tarnish it.

54: ♃ ♉ Royalty has manifested, one was handed a scepter. Learn how to rule, whatever the domain.

55: ♃ ♊ The skills of a powerful priest or priestess are present. Always remember the gravity of one's own words and actions upon others.

56: ♃ ♋ Much was sacrificed much for a king and queen. Seek another elegant task for added direction in life.

57: ♃ ♌ The essence of a knight lies within, the Universe has gifted one with royal momentum. Hold strong to a code of honor.

58: ♃ ♍ The life of the Hierophant or Queen Mother is sought after. Be cautious in one's advising, not all will welcome it.

59: ♃ ♎ The composure of a divine messenger is present. Be diligent in conveying messages and movements from a higher nature.

60: ♃ ♏ One has chosen to live by divine decrees and rules. Be true and obedient, but choose allegiances.

61: ♃ ♅ The only rule is that there is always an exception to the rule. Do not be ungrateful for any special treatment received.

62: ♃ ♐ There is a strong kinship and connection with the forests. Seek solitude among the trees for divine energy.

63: ♃ ♑ The flailing traits of a jester are present. Be tactful.

64: ♃ ♒ There is royal heritage, royal service, or a divine attendant in one's ancestry. On occasion, show honor to the universe.

65: ♃ ♓ The blood of a royal champion flows. Be magnanimous in victory.

♄: Saturn - Afterlife

66: ♄ ♈ One is on a journey on the other side. Discover what is needed in this realm to assist in that endeavor.

67: ♄ ♉ There is an aptitude for infusing items with sacredness. Always be on the lookout for unique spiritual items, places, and people.

68: ♄ ♊ There still exists a previous bond that survived death. Do not sever this tie without much deliberation, the other soul may still be in need.

69: ♄ ♋ One can hear spirits better than most. Be a good listener.

70: ♄ ♌ In the previous realm, one passed many trials. Rest and relax, for the next round begins soon.

71: ♄ ♍ A decision was made to come to this realm for a unique reason. Rely on wisdom, it can transcend.

72: ♄ ♎ One can see truth for the dead, they may come seeking it. Be patient with souls who are in pain.

73: ♄ ♏ There is a very mature soul that lived many lives. Do not let idleness creep in.

74: ♄ ♅ One can soothe troubled spirits. Be careful lingering in the realm of the dead too long, it can sow discord.

75: ♄ ♐ The last journey was peaceful. Remember those moments in times of difficulty.

76: ♄ ♑ Luck has a very strong influence on this journey. Be mindful of addiction and arrogance, but spread some wealth as well.

77: ♄ ♒ One's destiny is taking its course through more than one life. Seek divine assistance.

78: ♄ ♓ The past life was very turbulent. It is ok to ask others for comfort.

♅: Uranus - Dreams

79: ♅ ♈ Truth comes to light easier from dreams. Do not be ashamed of this method.

80: ♅ ♉ Identity comes into being much stronger in dreams. Learn how to stay true to oneself when not in that realm.

81: ♅ ♊ All matters and secrets about love can be learned and kept safe in dreams. Counsel others well.

82: ♅ ♋ One is tormented by dreams. Seek out others who are healers in that realm.

83: ♅ ♌ Trials and tests manifest themselves in dreams. Be sure to claim any rewards.

84: ♅ ♍ There is power over and through others in dreams. Abusing this skill will anger the rulers of that realm.

85: ♅ ♎ The skill of interpreting dreams comes easily. Offer others the insight learned, share the wisdom.

86: ♅ ♏ Truth stands apart from falsehoods within dreams. Seek out hidden knowledge there.

87: ♅ ♅ One can heal spirits in dreamland. Find others in need.

88: ♅ ♐ The waking forests and dreams are one and the same. Do not get too lost.

89: ♅ ♑ Dreams are treated as a playground. Enjoy the freedom, be calmed by them.

90: ♅ ♒ Destinies are easier to attain in dreams for some. Stay focused during the waking hours.

91: ♅ ♓ Attraction abounds in dreams. Seek advice from loved ones in the dream realm.

♆: Neptune - Boundaries

92: ♆ ♈ One can sense the unknown more than usual. Learn how to keep it at bay.

93: ♆ ♉ It is easy to find power beyond the walls. Find magic in large open spaces.

94: ♆ ♊ No bond is enough. Be strong in accepting things for what they are.

95: ♆ ♋ There is the ability to endure being lost for the sake of others. Rescue those who get lost and ask for help.

96: ♆ ♌ One likes to test all boundaries. Be reverent in these actions.

97: ♆ ♍ It is natural for some to set many boundaries. Always ask first if it is necessary.

98: ♆ ♎ Enough time has been spent beyond, there is knowledge of what is out there. Take extra time to ground.

99: ♆ ♏ One is a defender of boundaries. Remember that they are fluid and can change at any time.

100: ♆♅ Your strength will be your undoing in unknown realms, here is Asclepius proper. Heed the warnings and advice of others.

101: ♆♐ There is a love of being lost. Choose when to be a guide and when to be a pathfinder.

102: ♆♑ There is comfort on either side of the boundary, there is no fear. Do not judge others who do have fear.

103: ♆♒ Some order and purpose can be found in the unknown wilds. Let one's destiny stray into strange places.

104: ♆♓ One is set free on wild, beautiful, and exalting paths. Take someone along to share the wonder.

◇: Polar Point - Hidden Doorway

105: ◇♈ One carries the unknown with them. Be careful not to overwhelm others.

106: ◇♉ Harnessing shadows comes easy. Use them for their intended purposes.

107: ◇♊ Vulnerability can be a strength. Use this as an advantage to attract kind souls.

108: ◇♋ The choice was made to be blind to some matters. Reassemble the lost pieces of the soul, start a new path.

109: ◇♌ There is great skill at finding hidden doors. Document where they are and when they go to.

110: ◇ ♍ It is very easy to open hidden doors. Be mindful of others who are near when opening one.

111: ◇ ♎ The desires of the hermit are strong. Do not form unnecessary attachments.

112: ◇ ♏ Standing in the doorway grants power and purpose. Find those who unknowingly do wrong, show them the way through one.

113: ◇ ♅ Examining one's own limits shows new pathways. Be aware that the devil's advocate is not always needed.

114: ◇ ♐ One holds the keys to faery realms, hidden places reveal themselves in the woods. Learn new secrets.

115: ◇ ♑ No locks can stand in the way. Choose which doors to break open.

116: ◇ ♒ Destiny lies through another door. Learn the best times to travel back and forth.

117: ◇ ♓ Taboos are very subjective. Be more secretive than most.

△: **The Interactions**

⃝⟩ Accord: The outer planet's influence is at its height; it is receptive to offerings or prayers. Power is given by the outermost planet.

⃝< Antithesis: The best blessing is a curse, the pendulum of power swings both ways. Power has been taken by the outermost planet.

△ Constellation Boundary: There is great change, a border is being crossed. Actions are weighed.

⊔ Return: A new cycle begins. The nature of the planet shows the way.

Ɋ Court: Influence increases and then decreases. The outermost planet leads the way in combined affairs.

Ⲫ Audience: The planets wish to show their favor. Gifts from the universe will arrive and alter the course of life.

Ⲫ Assembly: Others arrive seeking judgment and wisdom. The planets may assist you during very dark moments.

◻O◻ Prominence: One was given tremendous independence and power from this constellation.

⊓ Void: The influences of the constellations in a void are lacking. Empty constellations may drain or weaken the soul if not tended to.

⊥ Sigil Crossover: Rivers will wind through each other on their way to the ocean. There will be many twists and turns.

╫ Quarters: Strength comes from sacred spaces or groves. Honor the divine with an altar.

The Elements

▽ Earth: There is a tendency to collect. Coalesce and manifest the physical.

△ Air: There is a tendency to think. Let the mind seek out truth.

△ Fire: There is a tendency to act. Allow experience and momentum to light the way.

▽ Water: There is a tendency to feel. Be fluid and guide through instinct.

The Elemental Currents

1: EE: Pure Earth, To ground. I came here to touch the earth. A landslide brought me here.

2: EA: Dust and sand, To storm. I came here to coat. The winds of a tornado brought me here.

3: EF: Charcoal and chalk, To draw graffiti. I came here to mark. The work of a painter brought me here.

4: EW: Clay, To constitute. I came here to shape. The work of a sculptor brought me here.

5: AA: Pure Air, To blow. I came here to journey. The wanderings of a traveler brought me here.

6: AF: Smoke and Ash, To darken. I came here to rage. The torrents of anger brought me here.

7: AW: Clouds, To precipitate. I came here to release. The winds of a thunderstorm brought me here.

8: FF: Pure Fire, To consume. I came here to encounter. The heat and light of a bonfire brought me here.

9: FW: Steam, To linger. I came here to perceive. The musings of observation brought me here.

10: WW: Pure Water, To flow. I came here to cleanse and revitalize. A soothing stream brought me here.

△ **The Eyes of Hyperion**

<u>Vantages</u>: Helios' Crown allows us To See.

V1: Midnight to 6 am. Eos appears. Gaze into dreams and memories.

V2: 6 am to Noon. Helios strides and focuses. Witness knowledge and strength in action.

V3: Noon to 6 pm. Helios slows and surveys. See matters that are settled and far away.

V4: 6 pm to Midnight. Nyx manifests. Peer into the darkness.

<u>Moon Phases</u>: Selene's Crown allows us To Sense.

MP1: Waxing Crescent and 1st Quarter: Selene is renewing. One imagines their own new path.

MP2: Waxing Gibbous and Full Moon: Selene is rejuvenated. One understands that no path is needed.

MP3: Waning Gibbous and 3rd Quarter: Selene is at rest. One is aware of the well-traveled path.

MP4: Waning Crescent and New Moon: Selene is in the shadows. One recognizes comfort on the empty path.

△ I: V1, MP1. There is joy in seeing paths unfold.

△ II: V1, MP2. The sight is strong into dreams and the past, what was forgotten.

△ III: V1, MP3. There is much that can be summoned for others from dreams.

△ IV: V1, MP4. It is easy to guide those who are lost.

△ V: V2, MP1. Elation is attained by finding the self in the wilds.

△ VI: V2, MP2. One seeks to test themselves in stillness.

△ VII: V2, MP3. Help from others is welcomed.

△ VIII: V2, MP4. One prefers to brave the strong winds alone.

△ IX: V3, MP1. A path to new lands is waiting to be found. One seeks a path that will tread new lands.

△ X: V3, MP2. One can see where paths end.

△ XI: V3, MP3. The best paths are recognizable.

△ XII: V3, MP4. The true self is found beyond borders/boundaries.

△ XIII: V4, MP1. Look for paths where others expect that there can be none.

△ XIV: V4, MP2. Absolute darkness can be dispelled by this soul.

△ XV: V4, MP3. Hidden figures can be seen clearly.

△ XVI: V4, MP4. There is much to be taken from the shadows.

NOTES:

NOTES:

NOTES:

NOTES:

NOTES:

NOTES: